Trient Press®

Trient Press
3375 S Rainbow Blvd
#81710, SMB 13135
Las Vegas, NV 89180

Ordering Information:
Quantity sales. Special discounts are available on quantity purchases by corporations, associations, and others. For details, contact the publisher at the address above.
Orders by U.S. trade bookstores and wholesalers. Please contact Trient Press: Tel: (775) 996-3844; or visit www.trientpress.com.

Printed in the United States of America

Publisher's Cataloging-in-Publication data
Trient Press
A title of a book : Trientrepreneur

What's Your M.E.S.S ?

Hosted By

Tracey D. Armstrong

Special Guest

It could be You...

What's your M.E.S.S.?

Mental.Emotional.Social.Status.
Takes you through the mess of
successful people's lives and
tells the backstory of when
their Mental, Emotional,
Social, Status of life was
a complete mess and
what they did to clean
up the messes in
their lives. .

Table of Contents

Trientrepreneur
magazine

Elevate Your Brand to New Heights:
Your Face Could Grace Our Inspiring Cover!

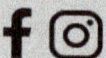
So, why wait? Take the leap, and let your brand's narrative intertwine with ours. Your journey towards innovation, leadership, and lasting impact begins with Trient Press Magazine. Your face on our cover could be the catalyst for a remarkable chapter in your brand's story.

Visit us at
www.treintpressmagazine.com

SOULFUL SELF-CARE:
NOURISHING SOLACE IN OCTOBER

Mindful Reflection: Take a moment each day for mindful reflection. This simple practice allows you to connect with your inner thoughts and emotions. It's akin to the introspection that characterizes the themes of October.

Nature Retreats: Consider spending time in nature, particularly in the midst of autumn's vibrant foliage. The changing colors and tranquility of the outdoors can serve as a wellspring of solace and inspiration. It deepens your connection with the natural world.

Candlelit Meditations: Incorporate candlelit meditations into your daily routine. The soft, flickering light of candles creates a serene and introspective ambiance, which aligns perfectly with the spirit of October.

Explore Mystical Literature: Dive into mystical or spiritual literature that resonates with you. These books, delving into the mysteries of the unknown, can offer solace through knowledge and insight.

Connect with Ancestral Roots: Use this time, when many traditions honor ancestors, to explore and connect with your ancestral heritage. Learning about your family history can provide grounding and enlightening experiences.

Create a Sacred Space:
Set up a dedicated space in your home for reflection and meditation. This personal sanctuary can be a refuge for moments of solace and introspection.

Autumnal Journaling:
Keep an autumnal journal to record your thoughts, feelings, and observations during this season. The act of writing can be a therapeutic means of finding solace in self-expression.

Celebrate Samhain:
Embrace the traditions of Samhain by participating in rituals or celebrations. These events can offer a sense of community and foster a deeper connection with the spiritual aspects of October.

Attend Mystery-Themed Events:
Explore events or lectures related to mysteries, folklore, or the supernatural. Engaging with like-minded individuals can create a sense of belonging and shared curiosity.

Practice Self-Care:
Always remember the importance of self-care. Prioritize activities that nurture your well-being, whether it's through meditation, exercise, or spending quality time with loved ones.

Assembly of Wanderers

Join us in navigating life's complexities, as we collectively shift from a reactive to a proactive mindset, replacing blame and expectation with gratitude and love, and realizing that within each of us lies the potential for unparalleled achievement, deep fulfillment, and a truly extraordinary quality of life.cumsan lacus vel facilisis.

WANDERCON

17-22 MARCH

FOR MORE INFORMATION VISIT : wandercon.assemblyofwanderers.com

Prepare to be inspired and transformed! Join us with a lineup of luminaries:
⭐ Master Trainer: Antonio T. Smith Jr.
🏈 Celebrity Speaker: Liffort Hobley
Keynote Maestros: Sheena Kerley, Deaunna Marie, Law Loadholt, and Tracey Armstrong.

An unparalleled assembly of brilliance awaits. Ensure your presence in this intellectual symposium—reserve swiftly, as seating is limited

Awaken your spirit, and enhance the beauty within.

 Instagram_ Account   Facebook_ Account   Twitter_ Account

PATH BENDER

By: Antonio T. Smith, Jr

HARDCOVER PRICE: $29.99

FIGHTING FOR MY LIFE TO WIN (PAPERBACK)

By: Arshisa Adejiyan

PRICE: $16.99

OFF THE PATH (PAPERBACK)

By: Tierell Goodman

PRICE: $24.99

RESILIENT SAILING (PAPERBACK)

By: Dr Carl M Barnes

PRICE: $28.26

NATURE'S PHARMACY : UNLOCKING THE POWER OF MEDICINAL HERBS

By: Deaunna M Smith

PRICE: $32.99

ARE YOU HAPPY : FINDING THE CEO IN YOU (HARDCOVER)

By: M.L.Ruscsak

PRICE: $29.99

EMBRACING LIFE'S UNCERTAINTIES:
Finding Strength in the Unknown

In the grand tapestry of existence, life's enigmatic mysteries often appear as dark shadows against the backdrop of our expectations. The human journey, with all its intricate twists and unforeseen turns, is an epic exploration of uncertainty. While our inclination may be to resist or fear the unknown, it is in this very ambiguity that we uncover profound opportunities for personal growth and resilience. In the spirit of embracing life's uncertainties, let us embark on a journey of enlightenment.

The Nature of Uncertainty

The word "uncertainty" itself carries a weight of unease, conjuring images of the unexpected and the unpredictable. Yet, it is this very quality that makes life an endlessly fascinating adventure. October, with its ethereal allure and ever-changing hues, serves as a poignant metaphor for the enigmatic nature of existence. In this month, when traditions around the world honor ancestral wisdom and engage with the supernatural, we find ourselves at the threshold of the unknown.

The Power of Vulnerability

To embrace life's uncertainties is to embrace vulnerability. It is a recognition that, at our core, we are fragile beings navigating a vast and intricate cosmos. Renowned psychologist and author Brené Brown elucidates that vulnerability is the birthplace of creativity, innovation, and change. It is the place from which we draw the strength to confront life's enigmas.

Consider the budding artist facing a blank canvas, the entrepreneur venturing into uncharted markets, or the traveler exploring unfamiliar territories. Each embodies vulnerability as they step into the abyss of the unknown. It is precisely in these moments of vulnerability that they find the wellspring of their strength.

Embrace the Unknown, for in Its Shadows Lie the Seeds of Growth and Resilience.

Resilience Through Adaptation

Adversity is the crucible through which resilience is forged. When life's mysteries unfurl in unexpected ways, we are presented with an opportunity to adapt and grow. The Chinese philosopher Lao Tzu aptly remarked, "Life is a series of natural and spontaneous changes. Don't resist them; that only creates sorrow. Let reality be reality. Let things flow naturally forward in whatever way they like."

Resilience is not the absence of adversity but the capacity to endure and thrive despite it. By navigating the unfamiliar, we hone our adaptability and cultivate a resilience that empowers us to weather life's storms with grace and determination.

The Role of Mindfulness

Mindfulness, an age-old practice rooted in the art of presence, becomes an invaluable tool on this journey. By embracing life's uncertainties with a mindful perspective, we learn to engage with the present moment without judgment. This heightened awareness enables us to perceive the hidden beauty within the unknown, transforming uncertainty into an opportunity for growth.

In October, the changing landscape mirrors the impermanence of life itself. The falling leaves, like our cherished plans and expectations, remind us that all things must eventually yield to change. Mindfulness teaches us to accept this reality with equanimity, finding strength in the impermanent nature of existence.

Conclusion: The Gift of Uncertainty

In the symphony of life, uncertainty plays a profound role, adding depth and richness to our experiences. It challenges our preconceptions and invites us to explore uncharted territories, both within and beyond ourselves. The mysteries of life are not to be feared but embraced, for within them lies the opportunity for personal growth and resilience.

As we traverse the intricate labyrinth of existence, let us remember that it is in facing the unknown that we discover the strength to evolve, adapt, and flourish. The path may be uncertain, but it is illuminated by the brilliance of our own resilience. In October's sacred shadows, we find not darkness, but the radiant light of possibility.

The Power of Ancestral Wisdom:
Drawing Inspiration
from the Past

Amidst the vast tapestry of human existence, a timeless thread remains unbroken and steadfast: our profound connection to the past. Ancestral wisdom, lovingly transmitted across generations in the form of stories, traditions, and cultural legacies, serves as a veritable treasure trove brimming with insight and inspiration. This repository of knowledge and guidance often slumbers, awaiting our recognition of its profound significance in shaping our lives. As we embark on this odyssey through the annals of ancestral wisdom, we uncover its transformative power, capable of shaping our present and charting our future.

The Tapestry of Ancestral Wisdom: A Universal Legacy of Collective Insight

Our human story is a kaleidoscope of cultures, experiences, and narratives, each thread interwoven with the next, creating a mesmerizing tapestry that spans across time. Within this intricate fabric of existence, ancestral wisdom stands as a luminous thread that refuses to fade. It is more than a mere collection of stories; it is a living, breathing legacy that encapsulates the collective wisdom of countless generations.

From the mesmerizing oral traditions of indigenous peoples, where wisdom was passed down through the spoken word, to the meticulously preserved written records of ancient civilizations, our forebears have bestowed upon us an incomparable

inheritance. This treasure trove of values, beliefs, and experiences is the culmination of human history and thought, a testament to our enduring quest for understanding and enlightenment.

At the heart of ancestral wisdom lies a profound belief: that the past, with its tapestry of struggles, triumphs, and hard-earned lessons, is an invaluable teacher for the present. It is a recognition that the trials faced by those who came before us are not mere footnotes in history but essential guideposts on our own journeys.

As we embark on the journey of delving into this repository of knowledge, we uncover an essential truth: ancestral wisdom knows no boundaries of time or place. It transcends the confines of cultures and civilizations, resonating as a universal compass for the human spirit. Its wisdom speaks to the hearts of people from every corner of the globe, binding us together in our shared humanity.

In these ancestral narratives, we find echoes of our own struggles and triumphs. We discover that the human experience, regardless of the era or location, is one of perseverance, resilience, and aspiration. The stories of courage in the face of adversity, the pursuit of justice, and the enduring quest for meaning traverse the boundaries of time, revealing our common humanity.

As we explore this tapestry of ancestral wisdom, we are invited not only to remember but to actively engage with the enduring lessons it offers. It is a call to listen to the whispers of the past and to heed the

the counsel of those who have walked this earth before us. Their voices, carried across time, guide us on our own quests for understanding, purpose, and fulfillment.

In the grand mosaic of human existence, ancestral wisdom remains an enduring beacon, illuminating our path through the ages. It is a testament to our shared legacy and a reminder that, regardless of the challenges we face, we are not alone. Our ancestors walk with us, their wisdom echoing through the corridors of time, offering us solace, inspiration, and a profound connection to the tapestry of humanity.

Drawing Inspiration from Ancestral Stories

Stories are the vessels through which ancestral wisdom flows most vividly into our lives. They are not mere narratives but vivid tapestries that capture the essence of our shared human experience. Ancestral stories often revolve around universal themes such as love, courage, resilience, and the pursuit of meaning.

These tales, whether they be the Greek myths of heroism and tragedy or the African folktales that convey profound life lessons, invite us to reflect upon our own experiences. They remind us that the human condition transcends time and culture.

By drawing inspiration from these stories, we find solace in the shared struggles and triumphs of our ancestors, knowing that we are part of an unbroken chain of human experience.

The Relevance of Ancestral Wisdom

In an era marked by rapid technological advancements and the ceaseless pursuit of progress, one might question the relevance of ancestral wisdom. However, it is precisely in our modern complexities that this wisdom finds its most profound resonance. Consider, for instance, the enduring wisdom of Confucius, who emphasized the importance of family, ethics, and social harmony. His teachings, rooted in ancient China, continue to resonate with individuals worldwide seeking guidance in navigating the complexities of contemporary life.

Ancestral wisdom often imparts enduring values that stand the test of time. These values include the importance of community, the significance of respect for nature, and the necessity of moral and ethical conduct. These principles, grounded in the experiences of countless generations, offer a moral compass for the present day.

Guidance for Modern Challenges

Ancestral wisdom provides a compass for navigating the intricate labyrinth of modern life. It offers guidance in times of uncertainty, reminding us that the challenges we face today are not unique to our generation. Our ancestors grappled with their own trials and tribulations, and their experiences serve as a source of strength and resilience.

Consider the wisdom found in Native American traditions, which emphasize the interconnectedness of all living beings and the need for harmony with nature. In an era marked by environmental concerns and ecological crises, these ancestral teachings offer a blueprint for a more sustainable and balanced existence.

Honoring Ancestral Wisdom

To honor ancestral wisdom is to pay homage to the resilience, ingenuity, and wisdom of those who came before us. It is a recognition that we are part of a grand narrative, a story that extends far beyond our individual lives.

One way to honor this wisdom is through rituals and ceremonies that acknowledge our ancestral roots. Whether it be celebrating traditional festivals, participating in cultural ceremonies, or simply sharing stories with family and friends, these acts of remembrance connect us to our heritage and provide a sense of continuity in an ever-changing world.

A Beacon in the Present

In the grand tapestry of existence, ancestral wisdom serves as a luminous thread that illuminates our path in the present. It offers us the opportunity to draw inspiration from the past, to find guidance in our most challenging moments, and to celebrate the enduring values that bind us as a global community.

As we navigate the complexities of modern life, let us not forget the timeless wisdom of our ancestors. Let us embrace their stories and traditions as a source of motivation, resilience, and inspiration. In doing so, we honor not only our heritage but also the boundless potential of the human spirit to transcend time and continue evolving through the ages.

Candlelight Serenity: October Meditations for Inner Peace

As the days grow shorter and the nights envelop us in their comforting embrace, October invites us to embark on a journey of introspection and inner peace. It is a month that resonates with the gentle flicker of candlelight, a symbol of serenity amidst the encroaching darkness. In this article, we explore the art of October meditations, guided by the soft glow of candles, as a path to rediscovering our inner equilibrium.

The Dance of Light and Shadow

In October, the world undergoes a subtle transformation. Leaves, once vibrant and green, now surrender to the allure of autumn, adorning the earth with a tapestry of fiery hues. It is a time of transition, where the boundary between light and shadow becomes more pronounced. Embracing this dance of contrast, we find an opportunity to embrace our own inner duality.

Candles, with their gentle illumination, become our companions in this journey. As we light them, we symbolically ignite the spark of mindfulness within ourselves. The flickering flame reminds us of the impermanence of all things and the ever-present interplay of light and darkness, both within and around us.

Setting the Scene

Creating the right ambiance is essential for a meditative experience that brings inner peace. Find a quiet space where you can sit comfortably, free from distractions. It could be a cozy corner of your home or a tranquil spot in nature. Arrange your surroundings to promote relaxation —a cushion or soft blanket to sit on, perhaps, or a chair that supports good posture. Ensure the lighting is gentle and soft; dim the ambient lights and allow the candlelight to take center stage.

Choose a candle, preferably unscented, as scents can sometimes be distracting during meditation. Place it on a stable surface in front of you, at eye level. Before lighting the candle, take a moment to appreciate its presence. Observe its shape, color, and texture. Feel the weight of the moment as you prepare to engage in this sacred practice. Now, with a mindful intention, carefully light the candle. As the flame springs to life, its warm glow invites you into a realm of inner exploration.

Engaging the Senses

Before delving into your meditation, engage your senses fully. Take a few moments to appreciate the flickering flame before you. Notice the play of light and shadow on the candle's surface, a reflection of the dance between tranquility and inner restlessness. Let the soft, ambient crackle of the flame draw you into the present moment. The gentle, warm light invites you to let go of external concerns and embrace the serenity of the here and now.

As you sit in front of this tiny beacon of light, allow your gaze to rest upon it without strain. Breathe deeply and inhale the subtle, calming aroma of the unlit candle. If you choose to use a scented candle, let its fragrance be delicate, akin to the scent of a gentle breeze or a fragrant garden. With each breath, let this aroma deepen your sense of presence, drawing you further into the tranquil space you've created. In this sanctuary of flickering light and soothing scents, you are prepared to embark on a journey of self-discovery and inner serenity.

"In the gentle flicker of candlelight, we find the wisdom of October: the art of embracing our inner dance of light and shadow. As days grow shorter, let us kindle the flame of mindfulness within, igniting a path to serenity amidst life's transitions. In the soft glow, we uncover the enduring truth: that inner peace, like the flickering flame, remains a constant, guiding us through the interplay of light and darkness within and around us."

The Flame of Intention

Now, set an intention for your meditation. What inner peace do you seek to cultivate? Is it a sense of calm, a release of anxiety, or a connection to your inner wisdom? Whisper this intention to the candle's flame, as if sharing a secret with an old friend.

Breathing in Serenity

Begin by taking deep, mindful breaths. Inhale slowly through your nose, allowing your lungs to fill completely. Exhale gently through your mouth, releasing any tension. As you breathe, let your gaze rest on the candle's flame. Observe its dance and the interplay of light and shadow. With each breath, imagine that you are inhaling serenity and exhaling stress. Let go of the worries and concerns that may have accumulated throughout the day. Visualize them dissipating like smoke into the air.

Guided Meditation

Close your eyes and continue to focus on your breath. Imagine yourself in a serene, natural setting, such as a peaceful forest or tranquil beach. Let the soothing sounds of nature envelop you. Allow your senses to fully immerse in this mental landscape.

Visualize a radiant light within your heart center. With each inhale, this light grows brighter and warmer. With each exhale, it expands, filling your entire being with a profound sense of peace and contentment.

The Dance of Inner Serenity

As you continue to meditate, envision the flame of the candle as a reflection of your inner self. It flickers and dances, mirroring the ebb and flow of your thoughts and emotions. Yet, beneath this ever-changing surface, there is a deep, unwavering core of serenity.

Let this meditation be a reminder that, like the candle's flame, your inner peace is always accessible, even amidst the turbulence of life's challenges. With practice, you can return to this place of serenity whenever you need to find balance and tranquility.

Closing the Meditation

As you conclude your meditation, take a gradual and mindful approach to reawakening to the world around you. Begin by slowly and gently opening your eyes. Allow your gaze to rest softly on the extinguished candle, appreciating the quiet reverence that has enveloped you.

Take a moment to bask in the stillness and peace that you have cultivated within yourself. Feel the residue of tranquility lingering in your heart, a testament to the power of inner serenity. This moment of reflection is an acknowledgment of the profound presence you've nurtured through the practice of candlelight meditation.

Now, as you prepare to re-enter the external world, gently blow out the candle's flame. Watch as the physical light dissipates, knowing that the inner flame of serenity you've kindled remains alive within you. With this act, you carry the essence of your meditation forward, a guiding light that illuminates your path in October's lengthening nights.

In the soft glow of the candle, you have discovered that serenity is not solely a reflection of the external world but a radiant presence that resides within your own heart, ready to guide you on your journey of inner peace.

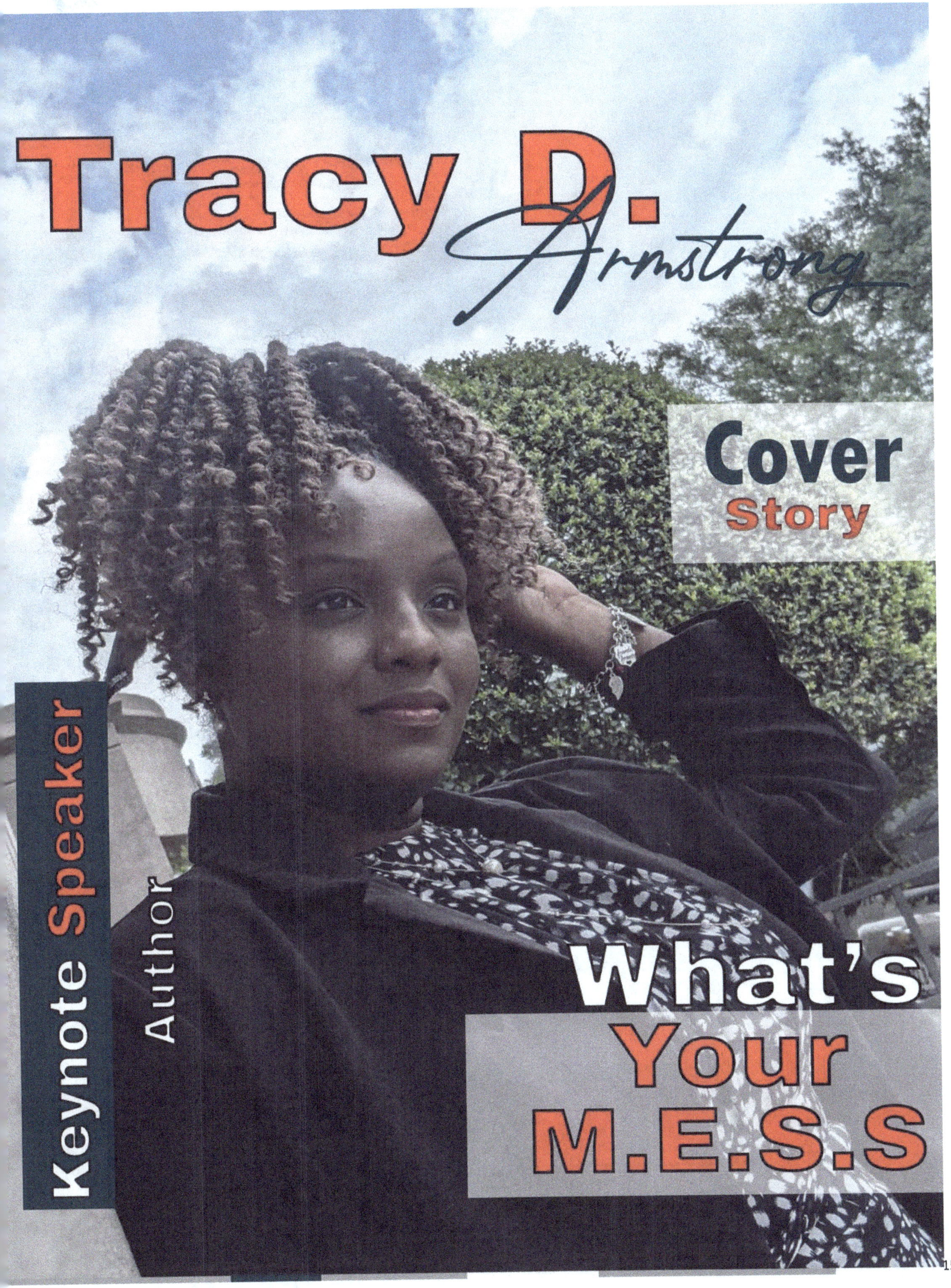

Tracy D. *Armstrong*

Keynote Speaker

Author

Cover **Story**

What's Your M.E.S.S

MARY J BLIGE

strength

WOL

Tracey D *Armstrong*

Born and raised in Houston, Texas, Tracey D. Armstrong's early life was marked by her mother's unwavering determination to raise an independent and self-sufficient woman. This upbringing instilled in Tracey the value of financial independence and the importance of providing for oneself without relying on others.

As she embarked on her educational journey, Tracey's background significantly influenced her career choices. Initially drawn to a career driven by financial prospects, she pursued a path in mathematics and accounting. Enrolling at Texas A&M University to pursue her MBA in Accounting reflected her initial focus on securing a financially stable future.

However, as she continued her studies, Tracey began to realize that her true calling lay beyond the world of numbers and spreadsheets. An innate inclination toward interpersonal connections and a deep desire to make a difference in people's lives led her to a pivotal moment in her academic journey. During her junior year, she made the courageous decision to change her major to Business Management. Notably, she completed her degree in Business Management within just four years, a testament to her dedication and determination.

Tracey D. Armstrong's career journey has been a testament to her unwavering determination and resilience. Starting her professional life with the JCPENNEY Corporation, she rapidly climbed the ranks, becoming an Assistant Manager at a thriving $25 million location. However, a sudden corporate transformation in 2012 led to her unexpected unemployment—a challenging period that would become a pivotal moment in her life.

In the face of adversity, Tracey displayed remarkable resilience. She swiftly secured a new opportunity as a Store Manager with Starbucks, where her management prowess contributed to the success of her store. Yet, she soon realized that her exceptional performance limited her prospects for further advancement within the company.

In a bold move in March 2015, Tracey took a leap of faith by resigning from Starbucks without another job lined up. Her unwavering determination to maintain financial independence and provide for her family drove her to complete her Teacher Certification courses in just three months. Her relentless pursuit of her goals bore fruit when she was hired at a nearby school, marking the inception of her educational career—a chapter that has significantly impacted her life.

WITHOUT PASSION LIFE IS NOTHING

Trailblazing Beyond the Classroom and Gym: Tracey D. Armstrong's Inspiring Journey

In the world of education and beyond, there are individuals who don't just follow a career path; they blaze a trail. One such remarkable figure is Tracey D. Armstrong, whose journey is marked by resilience, innovation, and a relentless pursuit of purpose.

Prosperity in Motion Cheer Company: In 2016, Armstrong founded Prosperity in Motion Cheer Company, a flourishing All-Star Cheer and Tumbling business. With dedication and a commitment to excellence, the company prospered until the unexpected challenge of COVID-19. Despite the hurdles, Armstrong's vision and leadership left an indelible mark on the world of cheerleading.

Author Extraordinaire: Armstrong's foray into writing showcased her multifaceted talents. Her book, "The Power of the P," stands as a testament to her ability to inspire individuals to lead productive, prosperous, and purposeful lives. Moreover, "Connecting Hearts," an E-Book she authored, offers valuable insights for mothers seeking to enhance their communication with their daughters—a true example of her commitment to building meaningful connections.

Podcast Host and Professional Speaker: As the host of "What's Your M.E.S.S.?," Armstrong dives into the messy, beautiful, and transformative aspects of life. Her engaging podcast invites listeners to explore their own paths, inspiring them to embrace their unique journeys.

All-Star Achievement: Armstrong's coaching journey reached a pinnacle when her All-Star Cheer team clinched victory at the U.S. Finals, a testament to her dedication and her goal of providing opportunities to athletes who might face financial barriers.

Coaching for Success: In a transformative shift, Armstrong transitioned from coaching teams to coaching coaches. Her expertise and leadership now empower coaches to elevate their skills, ultimately benefiting the athletes they train.

Trailblazing and Inspiring: Tracey D. Armstrong's career is marked not only by her personal achievements but also by her profound impact on the fields of cheerleading, communication, and personal development. Her journey serves as an inspiration, reminding us that with determination and a commitment to one's purpose, we can overcome obstacles and create lasting change. Tracey D. Armstrong is more than a name; she is a force of empowerment and positive transformation.

Join Tracey
MARCH 17-22
at Wandercon

Illuminating Minds and Transforming Lives

In a world often shrouded in doubt and negativity, individuals who radiate positivity and inspire transformation are like guiding stars. Tracey D. Armstrong is one such luminary, a beacon of hope and empowerment whose journey is nothing short of remarkable.

A Positive Visionary: Tracey's professional philosophy is grounded in the belief that transforming lives begins with transforming minds. She holds the key to unlocking the vast potential hidden within each of us. If you've ever doubted the power of a positive mindset, Tracey is here to remind us that it can pave the way for extraordinary possibilities in life.

Driven by Impact: What fuels Tracey's relentless drive is the desire to make a lasting impact on the lives of others. Her long-term goals align perfectly with this aspiration. She envisions herself speaking to millions in arenas across the globe, igniting sparks of hope and motivation in hearts that may have once felt dimmed. It's the stories of her students and those who have been touched by her words that fuel her passion to keep teaching and inspiring.

A Visionary for Prosperity: In Tracey's world, prosperity isn't just about wealth; it's about a rich and fulfilling life. Her vision for her field is clear—to encourage people to live lives that resonate with fulfillment and purpose. Through her message, she hopes to reignite hope in those who had given up, showing them that life has more to offer than they might have once believed.

Facing Challenges Head-On: Tracey acknowledges the challenges in her industry with grace and bravery. The need for visibility beyond one's usual circles and the courage to be vulnerable are not taken lightly. She knows that her journey isn't without its critics and naysayers, but she presses on, undeterred by the occasional storm, driven by her unwavering belief in the impact of her message.

Meet Tracey D. Armstrong: Tracey is more than a motivational speaker, more than an author, more than a podcast host—she is a catalyst for change, a guardian of positivity, and a guiding light for those navigating life's complexities. Her story, her philosophy, and her vision are not just inspiring; they're a call to action. To meet Tracey D. Armstrong is to glimpse the potential for transformation that resides within each of us. Her message is clear: embrace positivity, transform your mindset, and let your life radiate with fulfillment. Tracey D. Armstrong invites you to join her on this remarkable journey toward a more prosperous and purposeful life.

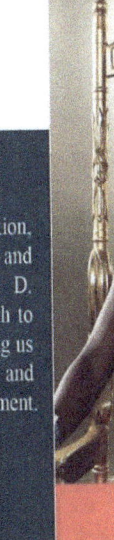

" In the realm of transformation, positivity is the catalyst, and mindset is the key. Tracey D. Armstrong illuminates the path to prosperity and purpose, guiding us to unlock our hidden potential and embrace a life rich with fulfillment.

50 & FOREVER

She's ICONIC

Navigating Challenges with Resilience and Impact

In the ever-evolving journey of life, challenges often appear as unexpected roadblocks, testing our mettle and resolve. For Tracey D. Armstrong, a renowned educator, author, and speaker, these challenges have become stepping stones to growth and resilience. As we delve into her remarkable career, we uncover the invaluable lessons she's learned from navigating adversity and the triumphant moments that continue to inspire her mission.

A Lesson in Communication: Tracey's path has seen its share of hurdles, including miscommunication and misunderstandings. In a digital age where words can be misconstrued, she once posed a simple question on social media that unintentionally led to a clash of perspectives. Her inquiry, meant to foster understanding, was perceived differently by others. Yet, it's precisely such moments that reveal the power of mindset and intention. Tracey's ability to approach these situations with openness and a willingness to learn highlights her resilience. She recognizes that fostering effective communication requires patience and a deeper understanding of others' perspectives.

The Triumph of Resilience: In Tracey's remarkable journey, resilience stands as a cornerstone of her character. She firmly believes that with the right mindset, any obstacle can be surmounted. Her unwavering spirit has not only helped her grow but has also become a source of inspiration for those she encounters. As an educator, her students often bear witness to her resilience and determination, instilling in them the belief that they, too, can overcome any challenge life presents.

Impact through Hope: Among the many rewarding moments in Tracey's career, there's one that shines as a testament to her unwavering commitment. A former student who had lost hope during her 7th-grade years, faced the world with newfound optimism after encountering Tracey's teachings. This student's transformation serves as a poignant reminder that a single spark of encouragement can ignite a lifetime of possibilities. Tracey's ability to instill hope in the hearts of her students showcases the profound impact she has on those she guides.

In Tracey D. Armstrong's story, we find resilience, optimism, and an unwavering commitment to making a difference. Her journey serves as a beacon of inspiration, reminding us that even in the face of adversity, there's an opportunity for growth, understanding, and transformation. Through her experiences, she empowers others to navigate life's challenges with grace and emerge triumphant, ready to embrace new horizons. Tracey's story beckons us to meet her, not just as an accomplished professional but as a beacon of hope and resilience in our ever-changing world.

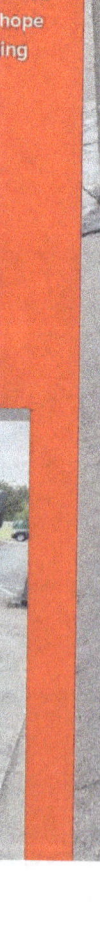

Shaping Lives and Leaving a Legacy

In a world that often celebrates individual success, Tracey D. Armstrong stands as a beacon of hope, dedicating her life to making a positive impact on her field, community, and beyond. As we delve into her journey, we uncover the multitude of ways in which she actively works to uplift and empower those around her.

Motivational Moments with TDA Mentorship: One of Tracey's most influential initiatives is "Motivational Moments with TDA Mentorship." Through this platform, she shares her wisdom, experiences, and insights with a broader audience. These moments of inspiration resonate not only with her students but with anyone seeking guidance on their life's journey. The power of her words is evident in the transformations she ignites in those who listen.

Free Webinars and Coaching Clinics: Tracey's commitment to community improvement extends to free webinars and coaching clinics. These educational resources serve as a valuable source of knowledge and skill enhancement. By offering her expertise and guidance freely, she empowers individuals and teams to reach their full potential. Her dedication to education and skill development reflects her unwavering belief in the power of knowledge to transform lives.

Philanthropic Ventures: Tracey's philanthropic endeavors extend even further through PMC All-Stars, her non-profit organization. PMC All-Stars is dedicated to raising funds for scholarships, ensuring that aspiring cheer and dance students can pursue higher education. Additionally, her involvement in "Counselors Corners" helps bridge the gap between students and parents on a social and emotional level, fostering a deeper understanding of one another.

A Beacon of
Inspiration and Impact

Quotes and Interviews:

Ask and it shall be given, Seek and yea shall find, Knock and the door shall be open to you. These powerful words echo Tracey's belief in the importance of taking initiative and pursuing one's desires. She instills this wisdom in her students and mentees, teaching them that opportunities often come to those who actively seek them.

"I can do ALL things through Christ who strengthens me." This scripture encapsulates Tracey's unwavering faith and resilience. It reminds her that with faith and determination, there are no limits to what one can achieve. This verse serves as a guiding light, propelling her forward even in the face of adversity.

"With God, ALL things are possible to those that believe and are called according to his riches." Tracey's faith is not just a personal belief but a driving force in her mission to inspire and uplift others. She exemplifies the power of faith in action, showing that it can move mountains and create lasting change.

Tracey D. Armstrong's journey is a testament to the transformative power of determination, faith, and unwavering belief in one's ability to make a difference. Her events are not merely gatherings but moments of profound inspiration and influence. As we conclude our exploration of her remarkable life, we can't help but be inspired by her commitment to shaping lives and leaving a lasting legacy of positivity and empowerment. Tracey D. Armstrong is not just a name; she is an embodiment of hope, resilience, and the limitless potential of the human spirit.

Closing Thoughts: A Legacy of Inspiration and Impact

In the closing chapters of this cover article, we have explored the extraordinary journey of Tracey D. Armstrong, a woman who has dedicated her life to igniting the flames of inspiration and impact. Her story is not just one of personal triumph but a testament to the boundless potential that resides within each of us.

As we reflect on the life of Tracey D. Armstrong, we are reminded that our journeys are not defined by the circumstances we encounter but by the resilience and determination with which we face them. She teaches us that adversity can be a stepping stone to greatness, and that every challenge is an opportunity for growth.

Tracey's commitment to her community, her unwavering faith, and her vision for a brighter, more prosperous world serve as a beacon of hope in an often uncertain world. She leaves us with a message that resonates deeply: with faith, perseverance, and a heart full of compassion, we can leave a lasting legacy of inspiration and impact.

In the pages of this article, we have barely scratched the surface of Tracey's remarkable journey. She is not just a woman of influence; she is a force of nature, an embodiment of hope, and a catalyst for change. As we conclude, we can't help but feel inspired to take action, to pursue our dreams, and to make a positive impact on the lives of those around us.

Tracey D. Armstrong's story is a reminder that each of us has the power to shape our destiny, influence our communities, and leave a legacy that transcends time. So, let us draw inspiration from her journey and strive to make our own mark on the world. In the end, it is not the magnitude of our actions that matters most but the sincerity of our hearts and the lasting impact we leave on others.

As we bid farewell to this cover article, let us carry with us the enduring message of Tracey D. Armstrong: that in the pursuit of our dreams and the service of others, we find the true meaning of a life well-lived.

TRACEY D. ARMSTRONG

AUTHOR·SPEAKER·EDUCATOR·COACH·MOTIVATOR

WWW.TRACEYDARMSTRONG.COM

Embark on a journey of wisdom and camaraderie at Dove and Dragon Radio. Tune in for riveting conversations spanning business strategies, travel tales, and more.

THE WORLD EVOLVES, RADIO TRANSFORMS.

WELCOME TO A NEW ERA OF AUDITORY EXPLORATION.

DOVE AND DRAGON
RADIO

FEAR AS A CATALYST: TRANSFORMING ANXIETY INTO COURAGE

In the intricate tapestry of human emotions, fear stands as a formidable thread, often weaving its way into our lives when we least expect it. It manifests in myriad forms: the fear of the unknown, the fear of failure, the fear of rejection. Yet, in the midst of this complex emotional landscape, fear holds a secret: it has the power to be a catalyst for profound personal transformation.

This article delves into the profound concept of fear as a catalyst, a force that, when acknowledged and confronted, can become a source of unparalleled courage and personal empowerment. Through the exploration of real-life stories and psychological insights, we embark on a journey to understand how fear, rather than a foe, can be a formidable friend on the path to self-discovery.

> " *In the loom of our emotions, fear is the thread that, when embraced, weaves the tapestry of our courage and personal transformation.* "

Embracing the Shadow of Fear

Fear, for many, is synonymous with discomfort and avoidance. It often compels us to retreat, to shy away from challenges and opportunities. Yet, psychologists and philosophers have long posited that within fear lies an extraordinary potential for growth. To confront fear is to confront our own vulnerabilities, to delve into the depths of our psyche, and to uncover the hidden reservoirs of courage.

Consider the story of Susan B., an aspiring artist who harbored an intense fear of rejection. For years, this fear stifled her creative expression, causing her to hide her artwork from the world. However, it was precisely this fear that propelled her to seek professional guidance and therapy. In confronting her fear of rejection head-on, she unearthed not only her latent artistic talents but also a profound resilience and determination to share her work with the world. Fear, in this instance, became the catalyst for her artistic awakening and empowerment.

The Alchemy of Fear and Courage

Fear, when channeled and understood, can transmute into courage—a powerful elixir that emboldens us to take risks and confront challenges. This transformation is not an easy process; it requires introspection, self-awareness, and a willingness to step into the discomfort of our fears. It is, in essence, an alchemical process of turning the lead of anxiety into the gold of courage.

Psychologist Carl Jung once said, "I had to recognize that I am not the master of the situation to which I am submitted; I must learn to bear the insolubilium." In acknowledging our fears, we recognize our limitations and vulnerabilities, and therein lies the first step toward personal growth. This recognition can lead to a profound shift in

Navigating the Unknown

Fear often arises in moments of uncertainty, when we confront the unknown. The fear of stepping into uncharted territory can be paralyzing, yet it is precisely in these moments that courage finds its most fertile ground. The unknown, as uncomfortable as it may be, is also where innovation and self-discovery flourish.

Consider the world of entrepreneurship, where the fear of failure is a constant companion. Entrepreneurs like Elon Musk and Sara Blakely are prime examples of individuals who embraced the unknown and transformed fear into courage. Musk, the visionary behind SpaceX, acknowledged the daunting challenge of space exploration and chose to venture into it despite the fear of failure. Blakely, the founder of Spanx, faced the fear of rejection when pitching her revolutionary product to major retailers. In both cases, fear served as a catalyst for innovation and groundbreaking success

Fear as a Wise Companion

As we navigate the intricate terrain of fear and courage, we come to realize that fear is not an adversary but a wise companion on our journey of self-discovery. When we summon the courage to confront our fears, we unlock hidden potentials, unveil our true selves, and find empowerment in the face of adversity.

Fear, transformed into courage, becomes a force that propels us forward, inspiring us to embrace the unknown, chase our dreams, and stand resilient in the face of life's challenges. It is the alchemy of fear and courage that leads to personal growth, empowerment, and a life lived to its fullest potential.

In acknowledging fear as a catalyst for transformation, we open the door to a profound shift in our relationship with this complex emotion. We discover that, in the crucible of fear, courage is forged, and our capacity for personal empowerment becomes limitless.

"In the dance between fear and courage, we find not adversaries, but companions in our odyssey of self-discovery. Fear, when met with courage, becomes the alchemist of our hidden potentials, revealing our true selves and kindling the fire of resilience in the face of adversity. This transformation fuels our journey toward a life lived boldly and authentically."

AMPLIFY YOUR INFLUENCE AND EMPOWER YOUR JOURNEY
WITH ATS LEADS

WELCOME TO ATS LEADS – YOUR POWERHOUSE FOR ELEVATING YOUR IMPACT IN THE WORLD.

Your Ultimate Lead Generation Solution! Get At Least 10,000 High-Quality and Tailored Leads a Month

MAXIMIZE YOUR SOCIAL MEDIA REACH:
DOMINATE GOOGLE WITH TARGETED HASHTAGS AND KEYWORDS:

SEIZE THE MOMENT TO EXPAND YOUR INFLUENCE AND EMPOWER LIVES

magine harnessing the vast resources of Google's expansive public database, the precision of social media platforms, the reach of targeted hashtags, and the specificity of email lists to connect with individuals eager to embark on transformative journeys with you. Discover a treasure trove of clients and mentees who are not just seeking guidance but are ready to embrace profound change. Seize the moment, share your wisdom, and watch your influence expand! 🌟📸

Join the ranks of mentors, life coaches, and spiritual leaders who have already harnessed the transformative power of ATS Leads.

Unlock your capacity to empower lives with ATS Leads. Seize the moment and witness your influence soar.

Are you prepared to amplify your impact and inspire meaningful change? Experience the dynamic capabilities of ATS Leads today!

PHONE: (409)-457-6304

WEB: https://atsleads.net/

BREAKING NEWS

Samhain: A Celtic Celebration

In the realm of ancient Celtic traditions, where nature and spirituality entwined in a harmonious dance, the festival of Samhain stood as a profound and sacred celebration. This age-old Celtic observance, with its roots firmly planted in the natural cycles of the Earth, has transcended time to influence the modern Halloween we know today. In this article, we embark on a journey through time and tradition to unravel the intricate tapestry of Samhain and discover how its legacy endures in the modern world.utate.

The Wheel of the Year: A Celtic Calendar

To understand Samhain, we must first grasp the concept of the Celtic Wheel of the Year. This ancient calendar, which delineates the agricultural and seasonal cycles of the Celtic lands, consists of eight festivals, or sabbats, evenly spaced throughout the year. Samhain marks one of these pivotal points, signaling the end of the harvest season and the descent into

The Celtic New Year

Samhain, often pronounced "sow-in," represents not only a seasonal shift but a spiritual one as well. It is regarded as the Celtic New Year, a time when the veil between the physical and spiritual worlds thins, allowing for a profound connection with ancestors and spirits. This belief endures in

Central to Samhain's significance is the Celtic reverence for ancestors. During this festival, it was believed that the souls of the deceased returned to visit their living descendants. To welcome and honor these spirits, families would set a place at their hearths, leave offerings of food, and light bonfires to guide the spirits on their journey. This tradition resonates with the modern custom of trick-or-treating, where offerings of sweets and treats are exchanged.

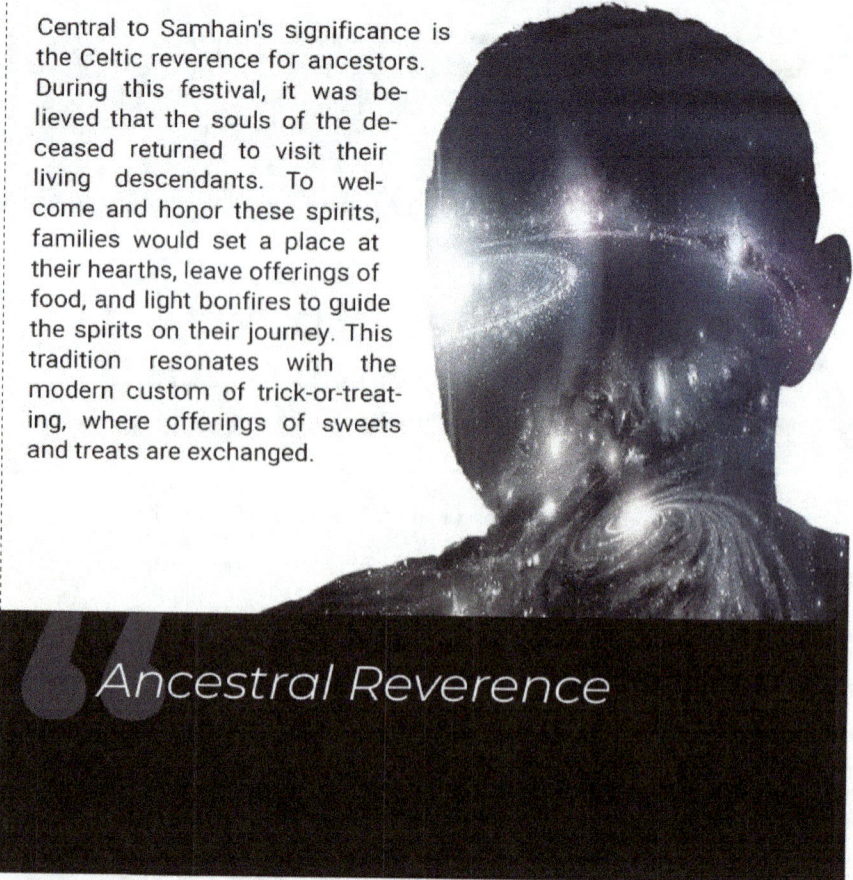

Ancestral Reverence

and the In-Between

Bonfires, an integral part of Samhain, served a dual purpose. Firstly, they symbolized the sun's waning power as the days grew shorter and the nights longer. Secondly, they were a means of protection against malevolent spirits that might roam the earth during this liminal time—between the end of one year and the beginning of the next. The bonfires we now associate with Halloween, often used to light up the night during festivities, hark back to this ancient practice.mattis.

— The Modern Halloween

As time marched on, the traditions of Samhain evolved, melding with other cultural practices and belief systems. With the advent of Christianity, for instance, Samhain merged with All Saints' Day and All Souls' Day, further intertwining its roots with the modern Halloween. Many customs, such as the carving of jack-o'-lanterns from turnips (later replaced by pumpkins in North America) to ward off evil spirits, have their origins in Samhain practices.

— A Legacy of Connection

In the ancient tapestry of Samhain, we discover a profound connection with nature, the spirit world, and our own ancestors. This Celtic celebration, with its rich traditions and deep spiritual significance, lives on in the modern Halloween festivities that continue to captivate hearts and imaginations.

As we embrace the playful spookiness of Halloween and engage in time-honored customs, let us also take a moment to acknowledge the ancient roots from which they spring. In the flickering candlelight and rustling leaves of this season, we find a thread that connects us to the wisdom and reverence of our Celtic ancestors, reminding us that, in celebrating Samhain, we honor not only the past but the eternal cycle of life itself.

SAMHAIN AND RENEWAL:

Harnessing the Energy of October

As the vibrant tapestry of autumnal colors blankets the Earth, and the crisp air carries the whispers of a changing season, we find ourselves in the embrace of October. For many, this month signifies more than pumpkin-spiced lattes and the rustling of fallen leaves; it holds the key to a profound transformation, rooted in the ancient Celtic festival of Samhain. In this article, we delve into the mystical energies of October and explore how Samhain can inspire us to reflect, release, and renew our goals and aspirations.

The Dance of the Seasons

To understand the significance of Samhain, we must first acknowledge the intrinsic connection between the natural world and human existence. Samhain, positioned at the crossroads of autumn and winter, is a festival that honors the cycle of life and death. The trees shed their leaves, the days grow shorter, and the Earth herself seems to exhale, preparing for a period of rest and rejuvenation. In this dance of the seasons, we discover a powerful metaphor for our own lives—a reminder that all things must come to an end to make way for new beginnings.

Reflection and Release

Central to the essence of Samhain is the act of reflection—a deep introspection that invites us to ponder the events and experiences of the past year. It is a time to acknowledge our triumphs and challenges, to celebrate our growth, and to honor the lessons we have learned. As the Celtic belief goes, by understanding our past, we gain wisdom for the future.

Yet, Samhain is not merely about reflection; it also encourages the act of release. It invites us to let go of what no longer serves us, to shed the metaphorical leaves of our own lives. Just as trees surrender their foliage to the earth, we can release old habits, negative thought patterns, and burdens that weigh us down. This act of release prepares the fertile ground for new beginnings.

THE CAULDRON OF RENEWAL

A Sacred Alchemy

In the rich tapestry of Celtic mythology, the cauldron emerges as a profound symbol of transformation and rebirth. This potent motif finds its embodiment in the mystical vessel of Cerridwen, the Welsh goddess of inspiration and transformation. Cerridwen's cauldron, often depicted as stirring with a magical brew, serves as a captivating metaphor for the alchemical processes of renewal and regeneration.

Cerridwen's Cauldron: A Source of Wisdom and Transformation

Cerridwen's cauldron is not merely a vessel; it is a font of divine wisdom and inspiration. In Celtic lore, the goddess brewed a concoction known as "Awen," a substance imbued with poetic and artistic inspiration. The act of stirring this cauldron symbolizes the transformative journey of the human spirit, the ceaseless stirring of experiences, emotions, and insights that shape our inner selves.

The Symbolism of the Cauldron

The cauldron itself is rich with symbolism. Its round shape mirrors the cyclical nature of existence—the eternal cycle of birth, death, and rebirth. The act of stirring signifies the ever-present change and transformation in our lives. Just as Cerridwen tended to her cauldron, we, too, are the keepers of our inner cauldrons, stirring the ingredients of our experiences to create something new and meaningful.

— Samhain and the Cauldron's Influence

During Samhain, the influence of Cerridwen's cauldron permeates the season. As the natural world transitions, shedding the old to make way for the new, we are invited to partake in this symbolic stirring. We can infuse our lives with the energy of transformation, rejuvenation, and renewal.

In our contemporary world, the traditions of Samhain may have evolved, but their essence remains potent and relevant. October is a time for us to embrace the energies of reflection, release, and renewal. We can take moments of solitude to contemplate our journey, express gratitude for what has been, and release what no longer serves us. In doing so, we create the fertile soil from which our dreams can spring forth.

As October unfolds with its vibrant colors and cool winds, let us remember the wisdom of Samhain—the wisdom that encourages us to honor the cycles of life, to reflect on our path, to release what holds us back, and to renew our hopes and aspirations. In this ancient festival, we find not only a celebration of the natural world but a powerful invitation to embark on a personal journey of transformation.

The Modern Relevance

PRACTICAL APPLICATION:

Renewal in Our Lives

In practical terms, this renewal can manifest as setting new intentions and clarifying our goals. Samhain encourages us to reflect on our journey thus far and consider the paths we wish to traverse in the coming year. It is a time for reaffirming our commitment to personal growth, much like the seeds of a new season committing to sprouting and flourishing.

In our daily lives, we can draw from the wisdom of Cerridwen's cauldron by embracing change, seeking personal transformation, and remaining open to the cycles of growth and renewal. Just as the goddess's brew of Awen brought inspiration, our renewal can lead to creative insights, profound self-discovery, and a deeper connection with our aspirations.

As October unfolds its autumnal splendor and Samhain draws near, let us remember the symbolic cauldron that stirs within us. It is a vessel of endless potential, offering us the chance to renew our intentions, clarify our purpose, and embrace the transformative energies of this enchanting season. In the spirit of Cerridwen's cauldron, we find not only the alchemy of self-renewal but a potent source of inspiration to shape our lives with intention and purpose.mattis.

SAMHAIN RITUAL:

Embracing Transformation

As the veil between worlds grows thin and the winds of October carry the wisdom of ages, it is time to honor the ancient Celtic festival of Samhain. In the spirit of Cerridwen's cauldron, we embark on a sacred ritual that embraces transformation and renewal. This ritual can be conducted alone or with a group, as you see fit.

Materials Needed:

A cauldron or a heatproof bowl
A small piece of paper and a pen
A lighter or matches
A quiet, sacred space
Preparation:

Choose a quiet and sacred space where you can perform the ritual undisturbed. Light a candle or several candles to create a sacred ambiance.

Place the cauldron or heatproof bowl in the center of your chosen space.

Have the small piece of paper and pen nearby.

THE RITUAL:

Begin by taking a few moments to center yourself. Close your eyes and take deep, mindful breaths. Inhale slowly through your nose and exhale gently through your mouth. As you breathe, envision yourself connecting with the energy of the season and the ancient wisdom of Samhain.

When you feel centered and present, open your eyes and pick up the piece of paper and pen. Reflect on the aspects of your life that you wish to transform or renew. These could be personal goals, habits, or areas where you seek growth and change.

Write down your intentions for transformation on the piece of paper. Be clear and specific about what you wish to release and what you hope to invite into your life during this season of renewal.

Carefully fold the paper, holding your intentions close to your heart. Visualize each word as a spark of energy, ready to be transformed in the cauldron of renewal.

With reverence and intention, light the folded paper from the candle's flame. As it begins to burn, place it in the cauldron or heatproof bowl.

As the paper burns, watch the flames dance and transform your written intentions into smoke and ash. Feel the release of old energies and the potential for new beginnings.

As the last embers of the paper fade away, take a moment to acknowledge the transformative power of this ritual. Sense the energy of renewal and growth that surrounds you.

Close the ritual with words of gratitude, either silently or aloud. You can express your thanks to the spirit of Samhain, to Cerridwen, or simply to the universe for the opportunity to embrace transformation.

Allow the candles to burn out on their own or extinguish them safely.

CLOSING THOUGHTS:

This Samhain ritual, inspired by the symbolism of Cerridwen's cauldron, is a beautiful way to embrace the energies of transformation and renewal that this season offers. As you continue your journey through the season of Samhain and the mysteries of October, may you find yourself enriched by the wisdom of ancient traditions and empowered by the potential for growth and change.

Finding Inspiration
Navigating the Mysteries of October

As October unfurls its mysterious and enchanting tapestry, it beckons us to embrace the sacred shadows that dance upon its canvas. This month, steeped in the traditions of Halloween and the ancient Celtic festival of Samhain, invites us to explore the profound connections between the present, the past, and the unseen realms. In this article, we embark on a journey to find inspiration amidst the sacred shadows, to navigate the mysteries of life with curiosity and reverence.

The Veil Between Worlds

In October, the boundary between the material and spiritual realms becomes thin, like gossamer threads woven by unseen hands. This phenomenon is a core theme of Halloween, where we acknowledge the presence of our ancestors and celebrate the interplay of light and darkness. It is a time to honor the mysteries that shroud our existence and to seek inspiration from the realms beyond our immediate perception.

The Ancestral Tapestry

One of the most profound sources of inspiration during this sacred season is the connection to our ancestors. All Hallows' Eve and Samhain both pay homage to those who came before us. By honoring our ancestors, we tap into a wellspring of wisdom, resilience, and guidance. Their stories, struggles, and triumphs offer a mirror to our own lives and remind us that we are part of an intricate and ever-evolving tapestry of existence.

The Dance of Light and Shadow

October's essence lies in its delicate balance of light and shadow. The vibrant colors of autumn are juxtaposed with the lengthening nights. It is a reminder that life itself is a dance between opposites—birth and death, joy and sorrow, certainty and mystery. By acknowledging and embracing these contrasts, we find inspiration in the richness of the human experience.

Cultivating Inspiration

To find inspiration amidst the sacred shadows of October, consider the following practices:

Ancestral Connection: Take time to learn about your family's history and traditions. Explore your ancestry and connect with the stories of your forebears. Their experiences may offer valuable insights and inspiration.

Nature Immersion: Spend time in nature, particularly in the changing landscapes of autumn. The beauty of the natural world during this season can be a wellspring of creative inspiration.

Creative Expression: Engage in creative activities that allow you to explore the mysteries of life. Writing, art, music, and storytelling are powerful tools for channeling inspiration.

Meditation and Reflection: Practice mindfulness and introspection. Use this time to contemplate the deeper questions of existence and seek inspiration from within.

Community and Celebration: Participate in community events or celebrations related to Halloween or Samhain. Engaging with like-minded individuals can foster a sense of connection and shared inspiration.

Embracing Life's Enigmatic Beauty in October

In the embrace of October, a season rich with sacred shadows and profound mysteries, we find ourselves immersed in the captivating dance of light and shadow. It is a month where the vivid colors of autumn leaves play against the backdrop of lengthening nights, reminding us of the enchanting interplay of contrasts that defines our human experience. Within this harmonious contradiction, inspiration unfurls like a tapestry woven with threads of curiosity and wonder.

As we traverse the intricate terrain of October, we also pay homage to the wisdom of our ancestors through All Hallows' Eve and Samhain. Their enduring connection to our journey whispers from the annals of time, offering guidance and resilience. In the stories etched in the tapestry of our forebears' lives, we discover threads of inspiration that seamlessly weave into our own narratives.

But the most profound source of inspiration lies in recognizing the profound interconnectedness of all things. October gently reminds us that we are not isolated beings but integral threads in the fabric of existence. Every action, every thought, every moment of reflection reverberates through the cosmos, infusing life with purpose and meaning. It is this awareness that breathes life into our inspiration, like a boundless river flowing from the heart of our existence.

In the hallowed embrace of October, inspiration flows not as a distant destination but as a timeless companion on our journey of self-discovery and wonder. As we navigate the sacred shadows and mysteries of existence, we discover that inspiration resides within, waiting to be awakened by our innate sense of curiosity, creativity, and awe.

The Resilience of Nature:

Lessons from Autumn's Transformative Beauty

As the summer sun mellows and the days grow shorter, the world around us undergoes a mesmerizing transformation. Nature, in its infinite wisdom, paints the canvas of the Earth with fiery hues of red, orange, and gold. The air carries a gentle chill, a reminder of the approaching winter. It's the season of autumn, a time of profound change and transformation, and nature's artistry provides us with valuable insights into our own lives.

In the midst of this vibrant spectacle, we find a powerful metaphor for embracing change and transformation in our personal journeys. Just as autumn gracefully sheds its leaves to make way for the new, we too can learn to let go of the old and embrace the beauty of transformation.

Embracing the Cycle of Change

Autumn teaches us that change is not an adversary to be feared but a natural part of life's cycle. The trees, once adorned with lush green leaves, surrender them to the wind. Yet, in their nakedness, they reveal a stunning vulnerability. This vulnerability, however, is not a sign of weakness but a testament to the courage of letting go.

Similarly, in our lives, we often cling to familiar patterns, relationships, or habits out of fear of the unknown. Autumn reminds us that letting go is an act of resilience, a declaration that we are willing to shed the old to make space for the new. It is through this process that we discover the strength to navigate life's changes with grace and poise.

A Time to Reflect and Realign

As we admire the autumn landscape, we are reminded of the importance of taking time to reflect on our own lives. Autumn invites us to pause, just as the trees shed their leaves, and consider :
What we are ready to release.
What habits or thought patterns no longer serve us?
What relationships or situations are in need of transformation?

By aligning ourselves with the rhythms of nature, we can find guidance in our own journeys. Autumn teaches us that embracing change is not a sign of weakness but a testament to our resilience. It encourages us to find beauty in impermanence, to savor each moment, and to believe in the promise of renewal.

As the world transforms around us, let us also transform within, embracing the lessons of autumn's transformative beauty.

OCTOBER'S AFFIRMATIONS:

EMBRACING CHANGE AND ABUNDANCE

As the leaves begin their graceful descent from the trees and the air takes on a crisper edge, October ushers in a season of transformation. Nature, in all its wisdom, invites us to embrace change with grace and enthusiasm. It's a time when the world around us undergoes a vibrant shift, painting landscapes with fiery hues, and reminding us of the beauty in letting go.

In this season of change, we become vessels of creativity, inspired by October's unique energy. Like the artist who draws inspiration from the evolving canvas of autumn, we too can tap into the wellspring of creativity that this month offers. Each falling leaf becomes a symbol of our own release—letting go of what no longer serves our growth, making space for fresh ideas and endeavors.

October also teaches us resilience, mirroring the adaptability of nature itself. Just as trees shed their leaves and stand sturdy against the approaching winter, we, too, can face life's changes with ease. It's a season that encourages us to find joy in the simple pleasures, relishing the crisp air and cozy sweaters that wrap us in comfort.

Amidst this transformative backdrop, we cultivate gratitude for the abundance in our lives, both seen and unseen. October whispers to us that trust in the natural flow of life is key, as we navigate the rhythm of the seasons and trust that everything unfolds in divine timing.

With these affirmations in hand, we become sources of warmth and positivity for those around us, radiating a light that shines even in the darkest moments. As October unfolds, let's open ourselves to new friendships and

01 *I embrace the changing seasons of life with grace and enthusiasm.*	**02** *I am a vessel of creativity, and October's energy fuels my inspiration.*	**03** *I am open to the mysteries of life and invite their wisdom into my journey.*	**04** *With each falling leaf, I release what no longer serves my growth.*	**05** *I am resilient, just like nature, and I adapt to life's changes with ease.*
06 *I find joy in the simple pleasures of autumn, like the crisp air and cozy sweaters.*	**07** *I am grateful for the abundance in my life, both seen and unseen.*	**08** *I trust in the natural flow of life, knowing that everything happens in divine timing.*	**09** *I am a source of warmth and comfort to those around me.*	**10** *I radiate positivity and attract positive experiences into my life.*
11 *I am grounded like the sturdy trees, deeply rooted in my values.*	**12** *I am deserving of love, happiness, and success in all aspects of my life.*	**13** *I embrace the unknown as an opportunity for growth and adventure.*	**14** *I am in tune with my intuition and trust my inner guidance.*	**15** *I am a beacon of light, shining even in the darkest moments.*
16 *I am open to new friendships and connections that enrich my life.*	**17** *I am mindful of my thoughts and choose positivity and optimism.*	**18** *I am a lifelong learner, constantly expanding my knowledge and wisdom.*	**19** *I am a magnet for abundance and financial prosperity.*	**20** *I am kind and compassionate to myself and others.*
21 *I am healthy and strong, nurturing my body and mind.*	**22** *I am a source of inspiration to those who cross my path.*	**23** *I am courageous and face my fears with determination.*	**24** *I am aligned with my purpose and live with passion and intention.*	**25** *I am in harmony with the cycles of life and embrace change with grace.*
26 *I am patient and trust that everything unfolds as it should.*	**27** *I am a source of peace and serenity in my own life and in the world.*	**28** *I am capable of achieving my goals and dreams.*	**29** *I am a force for good, making a positive impact in the world.*	**30** *I am grateful for the beauty and blessings that October brings into my life.*

Samhain Ritual

Honoring Ancestors
and
Welcoming the New Year

CELEBRATING SAMHAIN'S VEIL:

Ancestral whispers guide us as we welcome the new year's mysteries.

Tools You Will Need:

A small table or altar
A white candle (representing the Goddess)
A black candle (representing the God)
A bowl of water
A bowl of salt
A small offering plate with food and drink (such as bread and wine)
A small pumpkin or gourd (optional)
A photo or memento of deceased loved ones (op-

Preparation:

Find a quiet and comfortable space where you won't be disturbed.
Set up your altar with the white candle on the left, the black candle on the right, and the bowls of water and salt in the center.
Place the offering plate in front of the candles.
If you have a pumpkin or gourd, you can set it to the side of the altar.

SACRED SPACE AWAITS:

Prepare your altar, ignite your intentions, and let the veil between worlds grow thin.

Celestial Altar: A small table set with reverence, ready to hold the sacred space of our Samhain ritual.

Remembering Loved Ones: A heartfelt tribute with photos and mementos, honoring those who have passed beyond the veil.

The Ritual:

Cleansing: Begin by taking a few deep breaths to center yourself. Light the white candle, saying, "I light this candle to honor the Goddess and invite her presence into this space."

Casting the Circle: Stand and face the altar. Imagine a circle of white light forming around you, extending above and below. Envision this light as a protective barrier that separates this sacred space from the outside world.

Calling the Quarters: Starting in the east (representing air), say, "I call upon the element of air to be with us during this ritual." Continue to the south (representing fire), west (representing water), and north (representing earth), saying similar words for each element. Visualize each element's energy filling the circle.

Invocation of Deity: Light the black candle, saying, "I light this candle to honor the God and invite his presence into this space." Acknowledge the God and Goddess, speaking from your heart or using a prayer that resonates with you.

Honoring Ancestors: If you have a photo or memento of deceased loved ones, place it on the altar. Say their names aloud and express gratitude for their presence in your life. If you don't have an item, you can simply speak their names.

Offerings: Place a portion of the food and drink on the offering plate, saying, "I offer this sustenance to the spirits of my ancestors, may they find peace and nourishment in the realm beyond." You can also offer a small piece of the pumpkin or gourd, representing the harvest and the cycle of life and death.

Reflection: Take a moment to reflect on the past year. What have you learned? What do you want to release or leave behind as you move into the new year? Write down any intentions or reflections in a journal.

Closing: Thank the God and Goddess for their presence, saying, "Thank you for joining me in this Samhain ritual. As the wheel of the year turns, I welcome the new year with open arms."

Release the Circle: Visualize the protective circle of light fading away, returning the space to its normal state. Blow out the candles.

Feasting: Enjoy the food and drink on the offering plate, considering it a communion with your ancestors.

Final Thoughts: Take some time to journal or meditate on any insights or messages you may have received during the ritual.

This Samhain ritual is a simple yet powerful way to connect with the energies of the season, honor your ancestors, and welcome the new year with intention and gratitude. Feel free to adapt it to your personal beliefs and preferences.

The Nature of Darkness

Darkness can take many forms in our lives. It may be the loss of a loved one, the end of a significant relationship, a period of financial hardship, or even a global crisis that affects us all. Regardless of its origin, darkness has a way of enveloping us, obscuring our path, and leaving us with a sense of uncertainty.

EMBRACING DARKNESS:
FINDING LIGHT IN DIFFICULT TIMES

Life is a journey marked not only by joy and sunshine but also by moments of darkness and challenge. It is in these times of adversity that our inner strength and resilience are truly tested. While it's natural to shy away from difficult moments, there's a profound wisdom in embracing the darkness and seeking the light within.

Acknowledging the Shadows

In the midst of difficult times, it's often our natural instinct to push away negative emotions, hoping they will simply fade away. However, this resistance can inadvertently intensify our suffering. The first and crucial step toward finding light in these challenging moments is to acknowledge the darkness we're experiencing.

Acknowledging the darkness means allowing ourselves to fully feel the emotions that accompany difficult times. It means sitting with our pain, sadness, fear, or grief without judgment. This process can be uncomfortable, even painful, but it's an essential part of the healing journey.

When we deny or suppress our emotions, we bottle them up, and they can fester beneath the surface, affecting our mental and emotional well-being. This suppression often leads to further distress, anxiety, or even physical symptoms as our bodies attempt to cope with the unresolved emotions.

On the other hand, by confronting our emotions head-on, we create a space for healing and growth. We give ourselves permission to grieve, to feel lost, or to be afraid. In doing so, we acknowledge our humanity, our vulnerability, and our capacity to experience a wide range of emotions.

This acknowledgment is a powerful form of self-compassion. It's a way of saying to ourselves, "It's okay to feel this way. What I'm going through is challenging, and it's normal to have these emotions." This self-compassion is the foundation upon which healing and growth can begin.

When we allow ourselves to feel and express our emotions, we process them in a healthy way. It's as if we're releasing pent-up energy, making room for clarity and understanding. We start to make sense of what we're going through, and this understanding becomes a stepping stone toward finding the light in difficult times.

In essence, acknowledging the darkness is an act of self-empowerment. It's choosing to face our emotions, however uncomfortable they may be, and recognizing that they are part of our human experience. It's the first step on the path to healing, resilience, and ultimately, discovering the light that can guide us through even the darkest of moments.

Amidst the shadows, we seek the glimmer of hope, finding the light within ourselves.

THE LIGHT WITHIN

In the heart of darkness lies the potential for transformation. It's during these challenging periods that we often discover the depths of our inner strength and resilience. We tap into a wellspring of courage we might not have known existed. It's as if the darkness serves as a crucible, forging us into stronger, wiser individuals.

As we navigate the depths of adversity, we encounter opportunities for growth that we might not have otherwise recognized. It's through the struggle that we develop resilience, gaining the wisdom to face life's challenges with newfound courage and grace. Like a phoenix rising from its own ashes, we emerge from the darkness transformed, carrying the light of our experiences forward into the world.s.

Radiant in her resilience, she finds the light within, illuminating even the darkest of paths.

Seeking Support

While our inner strength is a powerful tool, it's essential to remember that we don't have to navigate the darkness alone. Seeking support from friends, family, or a therapist can provide invaluable guidance and comfort. Sharing our struggles with others not only lightens the emotional burden but also strengthens the bonds of connection.

In times of darkness, reaching out to those who care about our well-being can be an act of self-compassion. Their presence and understanding can illuminate our path and remind us that we are not alone in our journey. Whether through a heartfelt conversation, a comforting embrace, or the wisdom of a trained professional, seeking support is a courageous step towards finding the light within the darkness. Together, we can weather the storms of life and emerge stronger, guided by the collective strength of our support network.

Finding Meaning and Purpose

Difficult times can also prompt us to reevaluate our lives and priorities. They can lead us to discover a deeper sense of purpose and meaning. In the face of adversity, we often gain clarity about what truly matters to us. This newfound understanding can guide us toward a more fulfilling and purposeful path.

When we confront darkness, we are forced to examine our values, aspirations, and the legacy we hope to leave behind. This introspection can catalyze personal growth, inspiring us to make meaningful changes in our lives. We may find the courage to pursue long-held dreams, mend fractured relationships, or engage in acts of kindness and service to others. The darkness, paradoxically, can become a catalyst for transformation, pushing us to emerge from the shadows with a renewed sense of purpose and an unwavering commitment to live authentically and meaningfully.

As the sun's first light graces the forest, a hidden path emerges, guiding the way to a village of serenity and purpose.

THE ROLE OF MINDFULNESS

Mindfulness practices, such as meditation and deep breathing, can be instrumental in navigating difficult times. These techniques help us stay present and grounded, preventing us from becoming overwhelmed by fear or anxiety about the future. Mindfulness allows us to find moments of peace and clarity even amid life's storms.

Through mindfulness, we cultivate the ability to observe our thoughts and emotions without judgment. This non-reactive awareness enables us to respond to challenging situations with greater calm and wisdom. Rather than being consumed by negativity or despair, we can choose to approach difficulties as opportunities for growth and learning.

Moreover, mindfulness encourages us to connect with our inner resources of resilience and inner strength. It teaches us that we have the capacity to find serenity even in the midst of chaos. By practicing mindfulness regularly, we not only become more adept at navigating adversity but also discover the profound peace that dwells within us, waiting to be uncovered, even in the darkest of times.

FOR ADVERTISING AND COOPERATION, CALL +1 (775) 249-7401

EMBRACING CHANGE

In the depths of darkness, we find a profound lesson in the impermanence of life. Just as the seasons transition, and night yields to day, so too do our moments of adversity give way to new opportunities and personal growth. Embracing change becomes a cornerstone of our resilience, as we learn to navigate life's ever-shifting landscape with grace and adaptability.

Ultimately, the darkness teaches us that change is an inevitable part of life. Just as day turns into night, and winter gives way to spring, difficult times eventually transform into moments of growth and renewal. By embracing change and acknowledging the impermanence of all things, we become more resilient and adaptable individuals.

Embarking on a Journey Within: Exploring the Shadows of Self in the Enchanted Forest

Navigating the Shadows: A Journey Within

In the intricate tapestry of life, moments of darkness are threads that bind us all together. They come in various forms—loss, uncertainty, despair—and often catch us off guard. Yet, these shadows hold within them an opportunity for profound self-discovery and growth. The journey through darkness is not a linear path but a labyrinthine exploration of our innermost selves.

As we navigate these shadows, we confront aspects of ourselves that may have remained hidden in the light. The darkness acts as a mirror, reflecting our fears, vulnerabilities, and deepest desires. It is in facing these facets of our being that we truly come to understand and accept who we are. In doing so, we unearth reservoirs of resilience and courage that can guide us through the darkest of times.

Each step taken on this journey within is a testament to our willingness to confront the unknown and find the light within ourselves. It is an acknowledgment that, just as the night gives way to the dawn, so too can our inner darkness transform into a source of strength and wisdom. Embracing the shadows is an act of self-compassion, a commitment to our own growth, and a testament to the indomitable human spirit.

"In the heart of darkness, we uncover the strength to illuminate our path, for within the shadows lies the birthplace of our resilience, the canvas for our transformation, and the compass guiding us toward the light of purpose and growth."

Embracing darkness is not about celebrating pain or suffering but recognizing their role in the human experience. It's about finding the courage to face adversity, seeking the light within ourselves, and emerging from difficult times stronger and wiser. In these moments, we discover that even in the darkest of nights, the stars still shine, reminding us that there is light to be found in every corner of our lives.

The Power of Gratitude:
Cultivating a Positive Mindset

> "In the midst of life's chaos, the practice of gratitude becomes our steadfast anchor, grounding us in the beauty of the present and opening our hearts to the endless possibilities of a positive mindset."

In a world often consumed by the rush of daily life, where challenges and stressors can easily dominate our thoughts, the practice of gratitude emerges as a powerful tool for cultivating a positive mindset. It is a timeless wisdom that transcends cultures, religions, and backgrounds, uniting humanity in the

Gratitude, at its core, is the art of acknowledging and appreciating the goodness in our lives, both big and small. It is an exercise in mindfulness, a conscious choice to focus on the blessings that surround us rather than dwelling on what may be lacking. This simple shift in perspective has the profound ability to transform

Numerous studies in the field of psychology have illuminated the tangible benefits of practicing gratitude. From improved mental well-being to enhanced physical health, the act of counting one's blessings can lead to remarkable changes in our lives.

Expressing Gratitude

One of the most striking effects of gratitude is its impact on mental health. Research has shown that individuals who regularly engage in gratitude exercises experience reduced symptoms of depression and anxiety. By directing our attention towards positive aspects of life, we create a mental space where negativity struggles to thrive.

Furthermore, the cultivation of gratitude can enhance our overall life satisfaction. When we make a habit of recognizing and appreciating the goodness around us, we shift our focus away from the pursuit of material possessions or external validation. Instead, we find contentment in the richness of our experiences and relationships.

But the power of gratitude extends far beyond our mental and emotional well-being; it also influences our physical health. Studies have linked gratitude practices to improved sleep quality, reduced blood pressure, and strengthened immune systems. It seems that when we embrace gratitude, our bodies respond with enhanced vitality.

So, how can one harness the transformative power of gratitude in their daily life? The answer lies in simple yet intentional practices that can easily be incorporated into our routines.

Don't hesitate to express your gratitude to others. A heartfelt "thank you" can brighten someone's day and deepen your connections. Whether it's a kind gesture or a meaningful relationship, letting others know you appreciate them strengthens bonds and spreads positivity.

Mindful Reflection: Take time for mindful reflection, particularly during moments of challenge or stress. Instead of fixating on difficulties, pause and consciously identify things you are grateful for. This practice can provide much-needed perspective and resilience during tough times.

Random Acts of Kindness: Engage in random acts of kindness. Doing something thoughtful for someone else not only brightens their day but also fills your heart with gratitude for the ability to make a positive impact.

The power of gratitude is not confined to individual well-being; it ripples outward, affecting the communities we are part of. A society that embraces gratitude is more compassionate, empathetic, and harmonious. It's a reminder that in recognizing the beauty and goodness that surrounds us, we contribute to a world that thrives on positivity.

In closing, the power of gratitude is a timeless force that has the potential to transform our lives from within. It is a practice that transcends borders and unites us as human beings, reminding us of the profound beauty in the world. As we journey through life, let us embrace gratitude as a guiding light, illuminating our path towards a positive and fulfilling existence.

Turning Dreams into Reality:
Navigating the Unknown with Confidence

In the grand tapestry of life, our dreams often stand as the vivid threads that weave our aspirations and ambitions. They are the sparks that ignite our passions and fuel our pursuits. Yet, turning dreams into reality is a journey fraught with uncertainty, a winding path through the unknown. How do we navigate this terrain with confidence and resilience?

At the heart of every dream lies a vision—a tantalizing glimpse of a future we yearn to manifest. Whether it's a thriving business, an artistic masterpiece, or a life filled with purpose, our dreams beckon us to venture beyond our comfort zones. It's in the pursuit of these dreams that we truly discover ourselves and the boundless potential within.

The Visionary's Mindset

The journey from dream to reality begins with cultivating a visionary mindset. Visionaries possess a unique ability to see beyond the constraints of the present, to envision possibilities where others see obstacles. They embrace uncertainty as an essential part of growth and transformation.

One of the hallmarks of visionary thinking is the willingness to take calculated risks. The unknown can be a daunting place, but it is also where innovation thrives. Visionaries understand that setbacks are not failures but stepping stones toward success. They learn from each experience, using failures as valuable lessons on the path to their dreams.

The Power of Planning

While vision fuels our dreams, planning provides the roadmap to their realization. Turning dreams into reality requires a well-thought-out strategy—a series of actionable steps that bridge the gap between the present and the envisioned future.

Begin by setting clear, specific goals that align with your dream. Break these goals into manageable tasks, creating a timeline that propels you forward. Be adaptable, willing to adjust your plan as circumstances change. Flexibility is a key ally in the face of the unknown.

Remember that planning is not a rigid structure but a dynamic tool that evolves with your journey. Embrace the process of continuous improvement, refining your plan as you learn and grow.

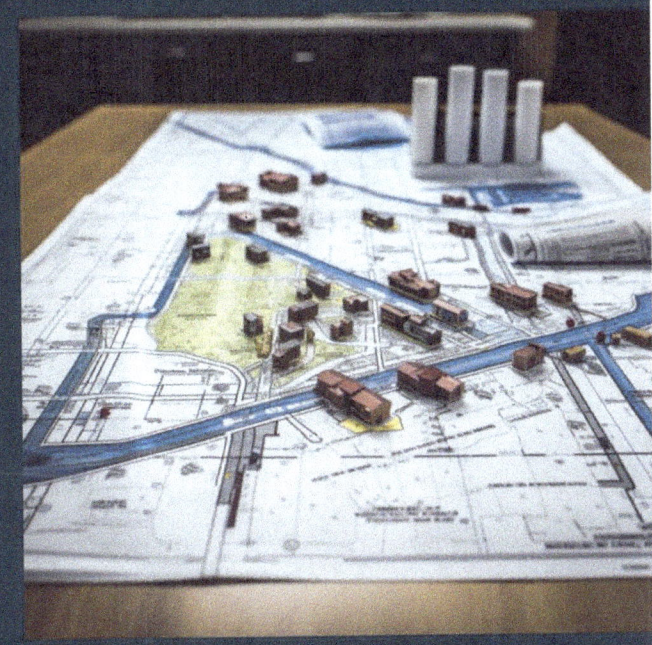

The Role of Resilience

As you embark on the path to your dreams, resilience becomes your steadfast companion. The unknown often presents challenges and setbacks, testing your determination and resolve. It is during these moments that resilience shines.

Resilience is not the absence of adversity but the ability to bounce back from it. It's the unwavering belief in your dream, even when circumstances seem insurmountable. Resilient individuals view setbacks as temporary detours, not dead ends.

A critical aspect of resilience is self-care. Nurturing your physical and emotional well-being ensures you have the strength to persevere. Engage in practices that rejuvenate your spirit, such as meditation, exercise, or spending time in nature.

Mulled Wine

Warm up with a glass of mulled wine, simmered with spices like cinnamon, cloves, and orange zest.

Ingredients:

1 bottle (750 ml) of red wine (choose a full-bodied wine like Merlot or Cabernet Sauvignon)

1/4 cup honey or sugar (adjust to taste)

1 orange, thinly sliced

1 lemon, thinly sliced

1 cinnamon stick

4-6 whole cloves

2-3 star anise pods

1-2 cardamom pods (optional)

1 vanilla bean (optional)

Additional orange and lemon slices for garnish

Cinnamon sticks for serving

Instructions:

Pour the red wine into a large saucepan or pot. Set the heat to low to medium-low, making sure not to boil the wine, as high heat can cause it to become bitter.

Add the honey or sugar to the wine. The amount you use depends on your taste preference. If you like it sweeter, you can add more.

Add the orange and lemon slices to the wine. These will infuse the wine with citrusy flavors.

Place the cinnamon stick, cloves, star anise pods, and cardamom pods (if using) into a small piece of cheesecloth or a tea infuser ball. This step makes it easier to remove the spices later and prevents them from floating in the wine.

If you're using a vanilla bean, split it lengthwise with a knife and scrape out the seeds. Add both the seeds and the empty pod to the wine mixture. This will give a subtle vanilla flavor.

Gently simmer the wine mixture for about 20-30 minutes, allowing the flavors to meld together. Stir occasionally.

Taste the mulled wine and adjust the sweetness by adding more honey or sugar if needed.

Once the mulled wine is fragrant and heated through (but not boiling), it's ready to serve.

To serve, ladle the mulled wine into heatproof glasses or mugs. Garnish each glass with an orange or lemon slice and a cinnamon stick.

Serve immediately while it's still warm and enjoy!

Mulled wine is a wonderful beverage to enjoy during the colder months, and its aromatic spices and citrus notes will fill your home with a cozy, inviting aroma. It's perfect for holiday gatherings or simply for unwinding by the fireplace. Cheers!

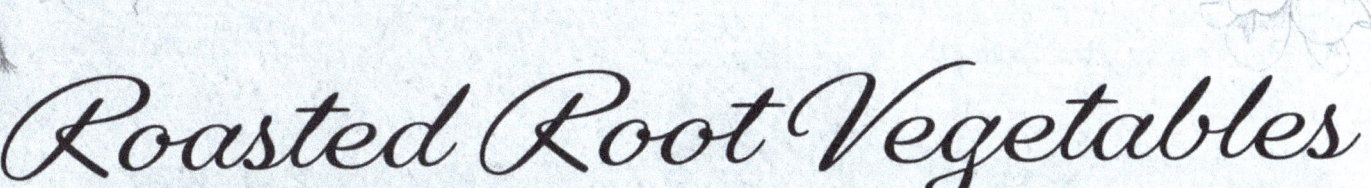

Roasted Root Vegetables

Ingredients:

4 cups of mixed root vegetables (carrots, parsnips, potatoes, and beets), peeled and cut into bite-sized pieces

2 tablespoons olive oil

2-3 sprigs fresh rosemary (or 1 teaspoon dried rosemary)

Salt and black pepper to taste

Instructions:

Preheat your oven to 425°F (220°C) and position a rack in the middle.

Wash, peel, and cut the root vegetables into roughly uniform bite-sized pieces. Keep in mind that denser vegetables like beets and potatoes may take a bit longer to cook, so you can cut them slightly smaller.

Place the prepared vegetables in a large mixing bowl.

Drizzle the olive oil over the vegetables. Make sure all the pieces are coated evenly with the oil.

Strip the rosemary leaves from the sprigs and chop them finely. If you're using dried rosemary, you can skip this step.

Sprinkle the chopped rosemary, salt, and black pepper over the vegetables. Toss everything together to ensure the seasonings are distributed evenly.

Line a baking sheet with parchment paper or lightly grease it with a thin layer of oil.

Spread the seasoned vegetables in a single layer on the baking sheet. This allows them to roast evenly.

Place the baking sheet in the preheated oven and roast for about 30-40 minutes. Check and stir the vegetables every 15 minutes to ensure even cooking. The total roasting time may vary depending on the size of your vegetable pieces, so adjust as needed. They should be caramelized, tender, and easily pierced with a fork when done.

Once the roasted root vegetables are done to your liking, remove them from the oven.

Serve the roasted root vegetables hot as a side dish. They pair wonderfully with a variety of main courses and add a burst of flavor to your meal.

Embracing the Shadows: A Haunting Dance of Light and Dark, Captured by Annibale Carracci. Explore the 5-Dimensional Depth of Fear and Fascination, Bathed in Eerie Candlelight, and Unveil the Unseen Terrors Lurking Just Beyond theShadows.

THE PSYCHOLOGY OF FEAR:
UNMASKING THE EMOTIONS BEHIND HALLOWEEN

As the leaves turn to fiery shades of red and orange, and the air takes on a crisp, cool edge, there's an undeniable sense of change in the atmosphere. For many, this time of year is marked by the anticipation of Halloween, a celebration that brings with it the thrill of haunted houses, eerie costumes, and tales of the supernatural. But what lies beneath the surface of our spooky traditions? What drives our fascination with fear during this season?

In this exploration of the psychology of fear, we will delve into the intricate web of emotions that underlie our love for Halloween and the unknown. From the rush of adrenaline to the comfort of communal fear, we'll uncover the reasons why we willingly subject ourselves to spine-tingling experiences.

Adrenaline Rush: Fear as a Natural High

One of the most significant psychological drivers of our love for Halloween fear is the adrenaline rush it provides. When we're scared, our bodies release adrenaline, a hormone that prepares us for the "fight or flight" response. Our hearts race, our senses sharpen, and our muscles tense in preparation for action. While we might not be facing real threats in a haunted house or horror movie, our bodies react as if we are.

This physiological response to fear can be addictive. The adrenaline surge can lead to a feeling of exhilaration, making us crave more of that heart-pounding excitement. It's a sensation many people find thrilling, like riding a roller coaster or participating in an extreme sport. Halloween serves as a sanctioned opportunity to seek out this sensation in a safe, controlled environment.

The Power of Catharsis: Confronting Our Inner Demons

Fear, in the context of Halloween, allows us to confront our inner demons in a controlled setting. The eerie monsters, haunted houses, and ghostly tales are metaphors for the fears and anxieties we carry within us. By facing these symbolic fears, we gain a sense of mastery and control over our own emotions. It's like practicing a psychological safety drill, allowing us to better cope with fear in our daily lives.

Psychologists refer to this process as catharsis, a release of pent-up emotions. Engaging with frightening scenarios during Halloween can provide a sense of relief and emotional cleansing. It allows us to temporarily escape from the stresses and anxieties of our everyday lives by channeling our fears into a shared experience with others.

Strength in Numbers: The Communal Aspect of Fear

Humans are inherently social creatures, and fear can be a powerful bonding agent. Halloween fear experiences are often shared with friends, family, or even strangers. When we scream together in a haunted house or watch a horror movie as a group, it creates a sense of unity and shared experience.

This communal aspect of fear can have a profound impact on our emotional well-being. It fosters a sense of belonging and connection, reinforcing social bonds. It's no wonder that Halloween is often seen as a time for parties and gatherings, as people come together to celebrate their shared fascination with fear.

> **"Fear is the master key to unlock the door to our deepest emotions. In the shadows of Halloween, we find not just fright, but the exhilaration of adrenaline, the catharsis of confronting inner demons, and the unity of shared fear. It's in embracing the psychology of fear that we discover the true magic of this eerie season."**

The psychology of fear is a complex tapestry of emotions, woven into the fabric of our Halloween traditions. From the thrill of adrenaline to the catharsis of confronting our inner fears and the sense of unity in communal fear, we find a multitude of reasons why we willingly embrace the eerie and unknown during this season.

So, as you prepare to don your spookiest costume or venture into a haunted maze, remember that there's more to Halloween fear than meets the eye. It's not just about the jump scares and eerie tales; it's about the shared experience, the rush of adrenaline, and the chance to confront our inner demons in a safe, communal setting. In the end, the psychology of fear reveals that Halloween

MADE YOU LOOK

WWW.TRIENTPRESSMAGAZINE.COM

 Unlock the Power of Knowledge with Trient Press

ARE YOU LOOKING FOR THE PERFECT PLATFORM TO SHOWCASE YOUR BUSINESS, PRODUCTS, OR SERVICES? LOOK NO FURTHER! [YOUR BUSINESS NAME] OFFERS PRIME ADVERTISING SPACE THAT REACHES A DIVERSE AND ENGAGED AUDIENCE.

DON'T MISS OUT ON THIS OPPORTUNITY TO SHINE! YOUR SUCCESS IS JUST AN AD AWAY. CONTACT US TODAY AT [YOUR CONTACT INFORMATION] AND LET'S START A CONVERSATION ABOUT HOW [YOUR BUSINESS NAME] CAN HELP YOU REACH YOUR GOALS.

WHY CHOOSE TRIENT PRESS?

✦ HIGH VISIBILITY: GET NOTICED BY OUR EXTENSIVE USER BASE FROM VARIOUS BACKGROUNDS AND INTERESTS.

✦ TAILORED EXPOSURE: TARGET YOUR AUDIENCE WITH PRECISION, ENSURING YOUR MESSAGE RESONATES.

✦ TRUSTED PLATFORM: BENEFIT FROM THE CREDIBILITY AND AUTHORITY OF A REPUTABLE SOURCE.

✦ BOOST YOUR BRAND: ELEVATE YOUR BUSINESS TO NEW HEIGHTS WITH STRATEGIC ADVERTISING.

🚀 **Your Business Could Be Here!** 🚀